BOLD KIDS

Porcupines

CHILDREN'S BOOK FILLED WITH FACTS

If you are looking for facts about Porcupines for kids, you've come to the right place. This book contains beautiful photographs of the species and interesting facts about this animal. The facts can help you complete school projects, as well as help you learn about the different kinds of porcupines in the world.

Here are some interesting facts about Porcupines for kids. We hope you enjoy it. It's a great resource for learning more about this amazing animal.

First, you should know that there are dozens of different species of Porcupines around the world. They originated in Africa and moved to South America 30 million years ago. Their habitats gradually changed and they eventually spread to both North and South America.

The North American Porcupine is the second largest rodent in North America, stretching from Alaska to Mexico. The scientific name for this species is Erethizon dorsatum.

The most fascinating fact about this species is that it is one of the largest rodents in the world. It has sharp quills that protect its young from predators.

Some of these quills are up to a foot long! The porcupine's prickly coat protects it from predation. This is also one of the reasons why they are so often mistaken for hedgehogs.

Although they don't have a gun, Porcupines have 300,000 quills. These are a defense mechanism because they can shoot them at predators. Fortunately, this means they don't shoot quills at their enemies, which can be quite frightening for children.

While porcupines' quills are extremely impressive, they can easily detach from their skin. This makes them an excellent option for kids to learn about animals.

The prickly coat of the African crested porcupine protects the animal from predators. This prickly coat is made of soft, dense fur. The porcupine's thick, spiky quills are an excellent way to protect itself from the predators.

Despite their large size, porcupines can survive in very cold climates, which makes them ideal for homes and farms.

The spiky quills of the porcupine help it defend itself against predators. The porcupine's long, hollow quills are responsible for its rattling behavior. The spiky quills on the back end of the animal help it rattle.

They are produced by the skin that covers the tail. During the rattling behavior, the porcupine also erects its quills, which is another great way to warn off potential predators.

The prickly appearance of a porcupine is not the only characteristic that makes it unique. This species has over 300,000 quills. Its quills are made of keratin and shed as new ones grow in. However, it does not shoot its quills.

The spines of the porcupine are attached to the skin loosely, and are easily detached by the spiky animal.

This spiky animal is the prickliest rodent in the world. Its Latin name means "quill pig." There are more than two dozen species of the porcupine. The quills are used to warn predators. Some of the quills are nearly a foot long.

Its tail can also be up to eight inches in length. So, if you are a parent or are planning to have a baby, facts about Porcupines for kids about the species of porcupines is a must.

The prickliest animal in the world is the porcupine. Its Latin name means "quill pig," and it's also one of the largest rodents in the world. Its quills are used to protect itself from predators. Some of the quills are almost a foot long.

While this animal has similar characteristics to other mammals, it is still very different in appearance and behavior.

It is important to note that the porcupine's name means "quill pig." The term refers to the animal's quills, which are soft, brown hair. The quills, which are made up of thousands of tiny barbs, cover the entire body of the porcupine except for the stomach.

The skin of the porcupine is covered with their quills, and the pig's back and behind are covered with the most, with the shortest ones on the face.

CPSIA information can be obtained
at www.ICGtesting.com
Printed in the USA
LVHW070830130123
737054LV00008B/125

9 781071 711293